the facts about
ELECTRICITY

Rebecca Hunter

First published in 2003 by Franklin Watts
Franklin Watts, 96 Leonard Street, London EC2A 4XD

Franklin Watts Australia
45–51 Huntley Street, Alexandria, NSW 2015
This edition published under license from Franklin Watts.
All rights reserved.

Copyright © 2003 Franklin Watts

Editor: Rebecca Hunter; Design: Keith Williams; Consultant:
Jeremy Bloomfield; Illustrations: Stefan Chabluk

Published in the United States by Smart Apple Media
1980 Lookout Drive, North Mankato, Minnesota 56003

Library of Congress Cataloging-in-Publication Data

Hunter, Rebecca, 1935–
The facts about electricity / by Rebecca Hunter.
p. cm. — (Science the facts)
Includes bibliographical references and index.
Contents: Electricity around us—Mains electricity—Cells and
batteries—Electrical circuits—Conductors and insulators—
Changing circuits—Circuit diagrams—Making electricity—
Clean electricity—Using electricity—Static electricity—Electric
animals—Electronic communications.
ISBN 1-58340-453-8
1. Electricity—Juvenile literature. [1. Electricity.] I. Title.

QC527.2.H86 2004
537—dc22   2003059088

9 8 7 6 5 4 3 2 1

Photographs:

British Nuclear Fuels: page 18; **Corbis**: cover, page 4, 6,
10 left, 16, 20 left, 21, 23 top; **Discovery Picture Library**:
page 7, 8 left, 10, 12, 14, 26 bottom; **Edison Mission
Energy**: page 21, 28; **Moor Park School**: page 29;
National Grid: page 12; **Oxford Scientific Films**: page 5
(Robin Bush), 20 right (Ronald Toms), 22 (David M Dennis),
24 (Warren Faidley), 27 (Max Gibbs); **Phillips**: page 9;
Science Photo Library: page 8 right (Martin Riedl), 10 right
(Chris Knapton), 13 and 19 (Martin Bond), 23 bottom (G
Brad Lewis), 26 top (Peter Scoones), 28 (Hencoup
Enterprises).

ELECTRICITY

Contents

Words in **bold** appear in the glossary on page 30.

Electricity around us

Electricity is a form of **energy**. It is very useful because it can be changed easily into other forms of energy.

Electricity has completely transformed the way people live. Only 150 years ago there were no electrical machines; now we can't imagine life without them. Electrical devices are all around us.

You can do it...

Count how many electrical devices you use in your day. Some are listed here, but there are many more. As a start, you could begin by counting how many electric machines you have in your house.

Electricity in your life

Think about how many times you use electricity every day. In the morning, you may be woken up by an electric alarm clock. You may turn on the radio and the lights—both are powered by electricity. For breakfast you might make a cup of cocoa, boiling the water in an electric kettle, and have some toast that has been made in an electric toaster. As you leave for school, you might listen to your personal stereo. The cars, trucks, and buses on the road all have electric **batteries**.

◀ We rely on electricity to provide us with many forms of entertainment.

4

▲ Auckland, New Zealand, at night.
Cities use huge amounts of electricity.

Schools, offices, shops, and factories are also powered by electricity. They contain electrical devices such as telephones, cash registers, and computers. At the end of the day, you might watch television or eat a meal cooked on an electric stove.

Electricity plays an important part in our lives. We cannot see it, but we can see what it does.

key facts

- Electricity is a form of energy.

- Electricity is used to power many machines.

- Without electricity our lives would be very different.

Mains electricity

The electricity we use in the home and at school is called mains, or current, electricity.

Mains electricity reaches your home through a wire. This is connected to a **power plant** which may be very far away. Mains electricity flows through wires in a similar way to water flowing through a hose. We call this flow an electric current. **Current electricity** is very easy to use because it can be sent along wires to wherever it is needed.

Electricity in the house

Once the electricity wire reaches your house, a set of smaller wires carries it through the walls, under the floors, and around the ceilings. Some wires carry electricity for the lights. Switches let you turn each light on and off.

▶ Electricity is carried across the countryside in wires that are strung between pylons.

Other wires go to outlets in the wall. You can connect electrical machines to these outlets using a plug with metal pins. When you push the pins into the outlet and switch it on, electricity flows through the plug and along the wire to the machine.

Mains electricity can be very dangerous. If it flows through the human body it will cause an electric shock that could be deadly.

▲ Both this stove top and microwave oven run on electricity. They have wires and plugs that connect to the mains electricity in the house.

key facts

○ Mains electricity moves in a similar way to a current of water.

○ Mains electricity is generated in power plants.

○ Mains electricity can be dangerous.

Safety

Follow these rules to stay safe from electricity:

- Never touch the bare metal of electrical wires. The wires should always be covered in plastic.
- Electrical outlets are for plugs only. NEVER stick anything else into an outlet.
- Do not use electrical machines near water.
- Do not touch light switches or plugs with wet hands.

Cells and batteries

Mains electricity is not the only kind of electricity. We can also get electricity from **cells** or batteries.

Mobile phones, radios, calculators, clocks, and flashlights need only a small amount of electricity. They get it from a cell filled with **chemicals**. When these chemicals **react** with each other they produce a small electric current.

Batteries

A battery is a group of cells that are joined together. The cells are placed next to each other in a casing.

▶ Many of the electrical items we use today are powered by batteries. This girl is talking on a cordless phone that contains a battery.

▲ Batteries for a flashlight or radio.

Voltage

The first battery was invented in 1800 by an Italian count, Alessandro Volta. The **volt**, the unit for measuring electrical force, is named after him. The power of a cell or battery is measured in volts. A small cell may give 1.5 volts of electricity. Cells can be connected together into batteries to provide more electricity. A small flashlight may use two 1.5-volt cells, so it has three volts. A radio may use a nine-volt battery that contains six 1.5-volt cells.

Uses of batteries

Small batteries are a much safer way to get electricity than mains electricity. They supply much less power and are not dangerous. Most batteries are small and light. This means the machines they power can be easily carried around. A personal stereo that had to be plugged into the wall would not be nearly as much fun!

Batteries come in many sizes. Watches and calculators use tiny, button-sized batteries. Flashlights and toys use batteries about the size of your thumb. Cars use large, heavy batteries to start their engines.

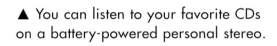

▲ You can listen to your favorite CDs on a battery-powered personal stereo.

Positive and negative

A battery has a positive and a negative terminal. In order to make the electricity flow, the terminals need to be joined together in a **circuit**.

key facts

- Electricity can be obtained from batteries.

- A battery is made up of a number of cells.

- The power of a battery is measured in volts.

Electrical circuits

A circuit is a circle that electricity can flow around. Electricity can only flow if the circuit is complete.

Several things are needed to make up an electrical circuit: a supply of electricity, connectors (to join the different parts together), and at least one **component** (something that uses electricity).

▲ All the lights on this Christmas tree are connected in a circuit.

▲ A close-up view of a light bulb. When it is connected to an electrical circuit, the filament glows brightly.

Every electrical circuit must get electricity from somewhere. In a simple circuit the electricity comes from a battery. You can join two or more batteries together to get more power. Metal wires connect all the parts of a circuit. They allow electricity to flow from one component to the next.

Circuit components

The circuit also needs something to use the electricity and show that the circuit is working. This could be a motor, a buzzer, or a light bulb. The wire inside a light bulb, called a filament, is very thin. When electricity passes through it, the filament glows.

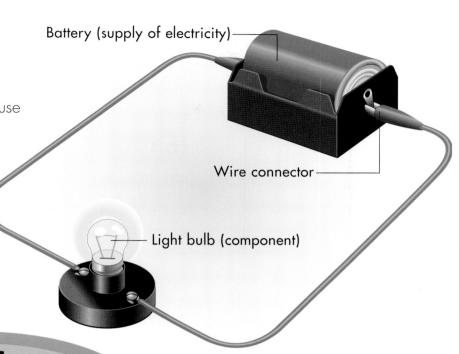

Battery (supply of electricity)

Wire connector

Light bulb (component)

You can do it...

Make a simple circuit. You will need a battery in a battery holder, a light bulb in a light bulb holder, and two wires. Attach a wire to each end of the battery holder, and then attach the wires to each side of the light bulb holder. If the circuit is complete, the light bulb will light up. Does your bulb light up? What happens if you break the circuit?

key facts

○ Electricity can flow only around a circuit.

○ A simple circuit needs a battery, two wires, and a light bulb.

○ If the circuit is broken, the electricity will not flow.

Conductors and insulators

Electricity can pass through some materials but not through others. Materials that electricity can pass through are called **conductors**. Those that block passing electricity are called **insulators**.

Conductors

All metals conduct electricity. That is why we use metal wires in circuits. Some metals are better conductors than others. Copper, aluminium, gold, and silver are all very good conductors. Electrical wire is usually made of copper, because it is cheap and easily available. Gold and silver are even better conductors, but it would be much too expensive to make wires out of them!

Insulators

Many materials do not conduct electricity. If something does not conduct electricity, it is called an insulator. Plastic, rubber, wood, and glass are all good insulators. All electrical wires should be insulated with a plastic coating to protect people from electric shocks.

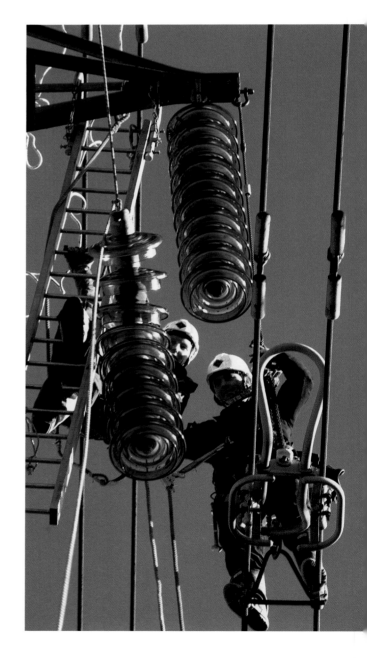

► Glass disks are used as insulators to hold power cables on electricity pylons. Thick glass is a very good insulator; it is also strong, durable, and weatherproof.

Test materials to see if they are conductors or insulators. Make up a simple circuit with three wires and leave a gap between two of them, as shown in the diagrams. Put the material to be tested in the gap and attach the two wires to it. If the material is a conductor of electricity, the bulb will light up. If the material is an insulator, the bulb will not glow.

▼ Plastic is an insulator. This plastic ruler will not conduct electricity, so the light bulb will not glow.

▼ If a metal object is used to connect the circuit, the light bulb glows. This shows the object is a conductor of electricity.

key facts

- ◯ Conductors are materials that allow electricity to pass through them.

- ◯ Insulators do not allow electricity to pass through them.

- ◯ All metals are conductors of electricity.

- ◯ Plastic, rubber, wood, and glass are good insulators.

Changing circuits

Several components can be added to a simple circuit to make it do more things or to control the flow of electricity.

Switches

Most circuits have a switch. A switch allows for the control of the flow of electricity in a circuit by switching it off. This is convenient and saves money, since most electric machines do not need to be on all the time.

You can add a switch to a simple circuit using a paper clip. This is done by cutting one of the wires and then screwing a paper clip on to a piece of wood.

▼ Switches around the house enable you to turn the lights on and off.

Attach the two ends of the wire to the screws underneath the paper clip, as shown in the diagram below. By moving the paper clip, you can either join the wires and allow the electricity to flow, or break the circuit and stop the electricity.

▲ Switch on: light bulb glows.

▲ Switch off: light bulb does not glow.

Adding more batteries

What would you expect to happen if you added more batteries to your circuit? When another battery is added to the circuit, more electricity flows through, making the light in the bulb brighter. But be careful not to add too many batteries or the bulb will "blow" (the filament will burn out and break).

▲ With two light bulbs, each bulb glows more faintly.

Adding more components

Light bulbs are the components in the simple circuits shown here, but you can also use others such as motors or buzzers.

▲ With two batteries, the light bulb glows brightly.

Adding more light bulbs

When you add more light bulbs to a simple circuit, the bulbs are dimmer because the same amount of electricity is having to light up more bulbs. If you want to put more components into a circuit, you will need to also add more batteries.

key facts

- Switches control the supply of electricity in a circuit.

- The more bulbs you add to a simple circuit, the dimmer each will be.

- Circuits can be changed by adding more batteries or more components.

Circuit diagrams

A **circuit diagram** is a map or plan of a circuit. Each of the components in the circuit has a **symbol** to represent it.

A circuit diagram shows whether or not a circuit will work. Scientists use circuit diagrams in order to work out what will happen when a circuit is changed.

Because it would be difficult each time to draw all the components in a circuit, scientists use symbols to represent them.

▶ This table shows the components in a circuit and the symbols used for them in a circuit diagram.

▼ Imagine what the circuit diagram for this department store would look like!

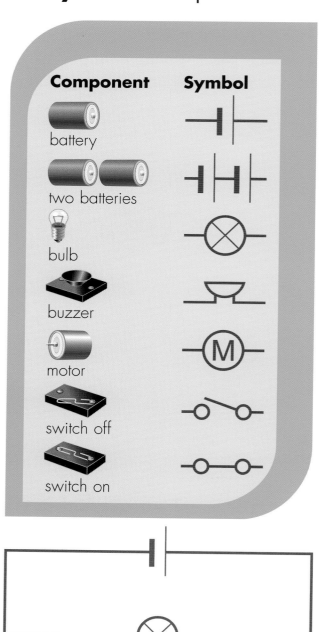

Component	Symbol
battery	
two batteries	
bulb	
buzzer	
motor	
switch off	
switch on	

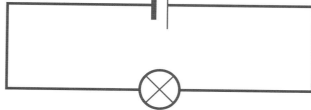

▲ This circuit diagram represents the simple circuit shown on page 11.

Can you tell which of the diagrams below represents the circuit shown on the right? (*You will find the answer on page 30.*)

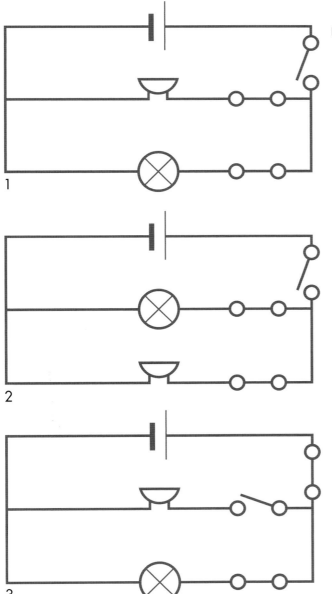

1

2

3

key facts

- Circuits can be drawn as diagrams.

- Each component of a circuit has a symbol.

- You can tell if a circuit will work by looking at its circuit diagram.

Making electricity

If a **magnet** is spun near a coil of wire, electricity is produced in the wire. This is how most electricity is made.

The dynamo

A dynamo changes movement energy into electrical energy. A bicycle dynamo has a small wheel that touches the wall of the bicycle tire. As the tire turns, the dynamo wheel is also turned. Inside the dynamo, the wheel is attached to a magnet. When the magnet spins, it produces an electric current in a coil of wire. It makes enough electricity to power the lights on the bicycle.

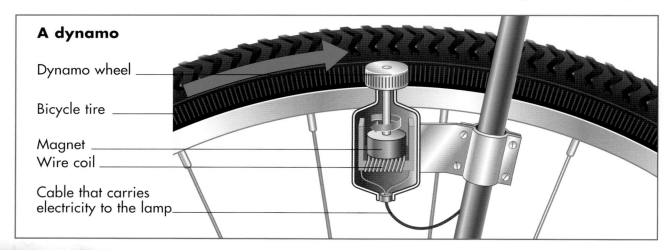

A dynamo

Dynamo wheel _____

Bicycle tire _____

Magnet _____
Wire coil _____

Cable that carries
electricity to the lamp_____

Generators

Most of the electricity we use is generated in power plants. It is made by powerful machines called **generators**.

◀ The interior of a power plant. Inside the large blue containers, turbines turn and generate the electricity.

▼ A coal-fired power plant. What looks like black smoke belching out from the towers is, in fact, harmless steam.

A generator is like a very large dynamo. Inside the power plant, water is heated to the boiling point and turned into steam. The steam drives **turbines** that rotate very quickly to produce electricity. The output of a power plant is 400,000 volts.

Electricity is carried around the country by heavy wires, often strung between pylons or buried underground. Devices called transformers reduce the voltage in stages to provide the level of supply required by various customers. The electricity used in shops, homes, and offices is 230 volts. That used by industry is 11,000 volts.

Fossil fuels

Most power plants burn fuels such as coal, oil, or natural gas. These are called **fossil fuels** because they are the remains of long-dead plants and animals. They are useful, high-energy fuels, but when they are burned they release a gas called carbon dioxide, which **pollutes** the air.

Another problem with fossil fuels is that they are being used up quickly. At the present rate, the world's supply will run out in about 250 years. That is why it is important to find new ways of making cleaner electricity.

key facts

- Electricity is made by converting movement energy into electrical energy.
- The machine that produces electricity is called a generator.
- The generators in most power plants run on fossil fuels.

Clean electricity

There are other ways of generating electricity. Many of these do not pollute the **environment** and are also **renewable**, which means they will not run out.

Electricity can be made using the power of the wind, the tides, the sun, and water. These methods are generally much less harmful to the environment than burning fossil fuels.

Solar power

Earth gets a huge amount of energy from the sun. **Solar energy** is non-polluting and renewable. Solar cells convert sunlight (solar energy) into electricity. Solar cells are found in solar-powered calculators, radio towers, and—in remote parts of the world—even public telephones.

◄ One of the big advantages of solar energy is that it can provide instant electricity in very remote places. Here, a solar-powered phone is being used in an isolated area of Arizona.

Solar cells are also used in space satellites and navigation buoys at sea. Some domestic homes now have solar panels on their roofs that provide them with "free" electricity.

Wind power

Wind power is another clean source of energy. Windmills have been used to grind corn and pump water for many centuries. Today, wind "farms" have hundreds of wind turbines that turn in the wind and generate electricity.

▼ These wind turbines are part of a wind farm near Palm Springs, California.

◄ The Hoover Dam HEP plant is built across the Colorado River in Nevada.

Geothermal energy is heat energy that is stored in the hot, molten rock deep underground. About 20 countries use geothermal energy as a source of heat or to generate electricity.

Tidal power is produced by holding back seawater at high tide and then letting it flow out through turbines at low tide. A tidal power plant at La Rance in France produces enough electricity for a city of 300,000 people.

Other energy sources

Other clean sources of energy include hydroelectric power, tidal power, and geothermal energy. About 20 percent of the world's energy comes from hydroelectric power (or HEP). This is power created by the movement of water.

In an HEP plant, a river is dammed to create a lake. When the water is allowed to flow through the dam, a generator changes the water's movement energy into electrical energy.

key facts

- Solar energy is one way of producing cleaner electricity.

- Hydroelectric power provides one-fifth of the world's electricity.

- Wind, sea tides, and geothermal heat can also be used to make electricity.

Using electricity

When we use electricity, we are converting electrical energy into other forms of energy: heat, light, sound, or movement.

Heat and light

One of the main ways we use electrical energy is to convert it into heat energy. When electricity is passed through a wire, the wire gets hot. The wires inside toasters and electric heaters glow red with heat.

Electricity produces light in just the same way. Light bulbs contain a thin wire, or filament, made of a metal called tungsten. When electricity is passed through the filament it glows white-hot, giving out light. The light bulb is filled with the gas argon, which stops the tungsten wire from burning up. Eventually, the filament becomes weak and snaps. Then the bulb "blows" and has to be replaced.

You can do it...

Look at a clear light bulb using a magnifying glass. Can you see how the tungsten filament is tightly coiled? The more coils there are, the brighter the light. The power of a light bulb is measured in watts (W). Household bulbs range between 25W (the dimmest) and 150W (the brightest). The power of the bulb is printed on the glass.

▲ On its own, an electric guitar is very quiet. The sounds are changed into electrical signals and made louder in an **amplifier**.

Sound

Televisions, stereos, radios, and computers all use electricity to produce sound. Today, one person can create the sound of a whole orchestra using just an electric keyboard and a computer.

Movement

Electric motors power many different machines. Washing machines, food processors, and lawn mowers are all motors that turn electricity into movement. Cars have electric motors to help them start and to work the windshield wipers. Research is being done to build cars that use only electricity, but at the moment they need enormous batteries to supply enough power for even a short journey.

key facts

- Electrical energy can be converted into heat, light, sound, and movement energy.

- Both heat and light are created by passing electricity through a wire.

- Scientists and inventors are working to build an electric car that can travel long distances.

◄ This prototype car is powered by electricity. It has batteries that can be charged and solar panels on its roof.

Static electricity

There is another kind of electricity called **static electricity**. Unlike current electricity, static electricity does not flow.

Making static electricity

Static electricity is caused by a build-up of electrical charges. There are two types of electrical charges: a positive charge and a negative charge. It is easy to see this in practice. If you rub a balloon against a fuzzy sweater, it becomes charged with electricity. The balloon gets a negative electric charge, while your sweater has a positive charge. If you let go of the balloon, it will stay attached to the sweater; this is because two differently charged objects are attracted to each other.

Thunderstorms

We can also see static electricity at work during a thunderstorm. Inside the storm clouds, pieces of ice and hail rub together and become charged with electricity. This is discharged as a flash of lightning.

Although we may only experience a thunderstorm a few times each year, Earth is actually being struck by lightning over 100 times a second!

▼ A dramatic lightning storm in Arizona.

Lightning conductor

You can do it...

See how like charges repel each other. Tie some cotton thread on two balloons and hang them together on a stick. Rub each balloon in turn on the same fuzzy sweater. What happens? Both balloons have the same static charge so they push each other away.

key facts

- Static electricity does not flow like current electricity.

- Static electricity is caused by a build-up of electrical charges.

- Lightning is caused by static electricity.

- Opposite charges attract each other, while like charges repel.

If the charges in the thunderstorm cloud are strong enough, the lightning can force a path through the air to the ground. Tall buildings, trees, and even people may be struck by the charge, which can carry up to 100 million volts of electricity. Many tall buildings such as churches have a metal pole on the roof called a lightning rod. This is connected to the ground. If lightning does strike, this conductor carries the charge harmlessly to the ground.

Electric animals

Electricity is not just seen in lightning or generated in power plants. It can also be produced by animals.

Nervous systems

Our bodies are run by electricity. Like all animals, we have a brain, which controls different parts of our body by receiving and sending electrical **impulses**, or signals, through our nerves. Every time we touch something, an electrical signal is sent through our nervous system to our brain.

▼ When you touch a cat, an electrical signal is sent to your brain. The brain tells you that the cat's fur is soft and pleasant to stroke.

▲ The Australian duck-billed platypus closes its ears and eyes when it dives. It searches for food under water using electrical signals, which it senses with its very sensitive bill.

Our brain then tells us what response to make. This all happens at very high speed. When you pick up a pan that is too hot, your brain tells you immediately to drop it.

The amount of electrical charge used in our bodies is very small, but some animals can make enough electricity to stun or even kill other animals.

The knife-fish

The Amazon knife-fish is a
very odd looking fish. It is
about eight inches (20 cm)
long and has only one fin
that runs all the way along the underside
of its body. Above this fin, buried under its
skin, is a line of **organs** that give out low-
voltage electrical impulses. These create
an area called an electric field. The knife-
fish can sense any small fish that swims
into this electric field and thus is able to
catch it easily.

The electric eel

The South American electric eel can
produce a massive electric shock of up to
600 volts that will kill or stun any fish
nearby. If you picked one up without
wearing rubber gloves or boots, the shock
would be enough to throw you flat on your
back. In some cases, horses standing in
shallow water have been knocked over by
the electricity produced by electric eels.

▲ The knife-fish produces low-voltage electrical
impulses used to catch its prey.

key facts

- All living things
  produce electricity in
  their bodies.

- Some animals use
  electricity to find and
  catch food.

- Fish can produce
  low-voltage electric
  fields or high-voltage
  electric shocks.

Electronic communications

Today, electricity makes it possible for us to not just talk to someone on the other side of the world, but to send them messages and pictures instantly.

Electronic equipment changes sounds and pictures into electricity and sends them at amazing speed, even around the world. When they reach their destination, they are changed back into sounds and pictures by other electronic equipment. All electronic communication needs a device called a **transmitter** to send out the information, something to carry the signals, and a **receiver** to change the signals back into a form we can understand.

The telephone

The first telephone was built in 1876 by Alexander Graham Bell. Bell was a teacher of deaf people and was interested in trying to change speech into electrical signals that could be sent down a wire.

When you dial a number, the dialing tones pass along wires to your local telephone exchange. You will then be connected with an exchange in the area that you are calling. You may sometimes notice a slight delay when talking to someone overseas. This is because your call is going via a satellite in space! Huge dish-shaped antennae on the ground transmit the signals up to the satellite. The solar-powered satellite beams the signals back to an antenna in another part of the world.

▼ This satellite dish is part of NASA's Deep Space Network. It tracks and communicates with satellites and space-craft throughout the solar system.

▲ Most schools are now connected to the Internet, giving students access to vast quantities of information on almost every subject.

The Internet

One of the most important modern electronic communication devices is the Internet. The Internet is a world-wide network of computers connected by high-speed telephone links. Using the Internet, which is powered by electricity, it is now possible to get information on any subject almost instantly, from anywhere in the world.

key facts

- Electricity is used in many forms of telecommunication.

- Telephones, the Internet, radios, televisions, and computers all need electricity in order to work.

Glossary

Amplifier A machine that increases the loudness of sounds.

Battery A battery stores electricity. It is made up of several cells.

Cell A container that holds chemicals that make electricity flow through a circuit.

Chemicals Substances that can be found naturally or manufactured.

Circuit The circle containing wires, components, and a battery, through which electricity flows.

Circuit diagram Plan of a circuit that uses symbols to show all the components in a circuit and how they are connected.

Component A device in a circuit.

Conductor Something that allows electricity to flow through it easily.

Current electricity Electricity that flows through a wire or cable.

Energy What people, animals, and machines need to give them the power to do work.

Environment The surroundings that make up the place where you live.

Fossil fuels The fuels coal, oil, and natural gas. All are obtained from the fossilized remains of plants and animals that lived millions of years ago.

Generator A machine at a power plant that turns movement energy into electrical energy.

Impulse A short push or surge of energy.

Insulator Something that does not allow electricity to flow through it.

Magnet A piece of iron that attracts other pieces of iron or steel towards it.

Organs Internal parts of the body that perform different functions.

Pollute To make something dirty.

Power plant A place that generates, or makes, electricity.

React To change because of something that has happened.

Receiver A device for receiving messages.

Renewable Describes something that you can always get more of.

Solar energy Energy from the sun.

Static electricity Electricity that builds up on objects rubbed together. Static means "not moving."

Symbol A shape or picture that is used to represent something.

Transmitter A device that is used to transmit, or send, messages.

Turbine A machine that is made to rotate and drive a generator.

Volt/voltage The measure of the force of an electric current or the power of a battery.

Answer: Circuit diagram 3 represents the circuit shown on page 17.

Further information

Books

Cooper, Christopher. *Electricity: From Amps to Volts*. Portsmouth, New Hampshire: Heinemann Library, 2003.

Good, Keith. *Zap It!: Exciting Electricity Activities*. Minneapolis: Lerner Publications, 2003.

Tagliaferro, Linda. *Thomas Edison: Inventor of the Age of Electricity*. Minneapolis: Lerner Publications, 2003.

Williams, Brian. *Faraday: Pioneer of Electricity*. Hauppauge New York: Barrons, 2003.

Web sites

Science Made Simple: Static Electricity
Easy to read description of the phenomenon, plus fun projects you can do at home.
http://www.sciencemadesimple.com/static.html

Hydroelectric Power
Describes how water's mechanical energy is turned into electricity. From the National Renewable Energy Laboratory.
http://www.nrel.gov/lab/pao/hydroelectric.html

How do you make electricity?
Find out how by asking Earl!
http://www.yahooligans.com/content/ask_earl/20020523.html

BrainPOP: Electricity
Watch cartoons, do quizzes, and try experiments about electricity and related topics such as thunderstorms, batteries, and other energy sources.
http://www.brainpop.com/science/electricity/

Electricity Online
Learn all about electricity, its applications, and its history. Features experiments, activities, and an historical timeline.
http://library.thinkquest.org/28032/

Places to Visit

U.S.
American Museum of Natural History
New York City, New York
http://www.amnh.org

Field Museum of Natural History
Chicago, Illinois
http://www.fieldmuseum.org

Museum of Science and Industry
Chicago, Illinois
http://www.msichicago.org

Pacific Science Center
Seattle, Washington
http://www.pacsci.org

Science Museum of Minnesota
St. Paul, Minnesota
http://www.smm.org

Smithsonian Institution
Washington, DC
http://www.si.edu

Canada
Canada Science and Technology Museum
Ottawa, Ontario
http://www.sciencetech.technomuses.ca

Provincial Museum of Alberta
Edmonton, Alberta
http://www.pma.edmonton.ab.ca

Index